Insurance Industry
Suspicious Activity Reporting

An Assessment of
Suspicious Activity Report Filings
April 2008

Insurance Industry

Suspicious Activity Reporting

An Assessment of
Suspicious Activity Report Filings

April 2008

Table of Contents

Purpose

This report highlights key findings of an assessment conducted by the Financial Crimes Enforcement Network (FinCEN) of Suspicious Activity Report (SAR) filings in the one-year period from May 2, 2006 through May 1, 2007 by insurance companies regarding suspected money laundering and other financial crimes. FinCEN conducted this assessment for filings by this industry, which is relatively new to anti-money laundering (AML) compliance, to identify typologies, trends and patterns relating to filing volume, filer location, subject location and occupation, characterizations of suspected crimes, and other factors relevant to the reporting of suspicious activity on a variety of insurance products. This report includes summaries of actual SAR narratives, revealing potential money laundering trends and frequently reported money laundering schemes. This report also includes preliminary observations regarding SARs filed from May 2007 through October 2007. Consistent with FinCEN's mission to provide beneficial information to law enforcement, regulators and regulated industries, this report will present indicia of possible illicit activity that some insurance companies have identified, and hence raise awareness of possible risks and vulnerabilities.

This report offers insight into the quality of the reporting. SAR narratives should make available clear, concise and invaluable information to law enforcement investigators. The relatively new reporting requirements on certain segments of the insurance industry provide an opportunity for an early evaluation of the quantity, quality and substance of existing filings. This opportunity for feedback to the industry can promote better information for law enforcement and will help establish a foundation to shape FinCEN's future analysis and guidance efforts.

Executive Summary

F inCEN is committed to providing quality written feedback to industries affected by new or changed regulations. The optional requirement for certain insurance companies to file SARs regarding some covered products became mandatory in May 2006. FinCEN previously issued brief reports concerning SARs filed by the insurance industry in February 2003 and again in May 2007. This report provides a more in-depth review of insurance company SAR filings and will serve to provide a baseline for future comparisons.

Overall, the quality of SAR reporting has been quite good, indicating that insurance companies are well positioned to report to law enforcement several specific categories of suspected illicit activities relating to money laundering. In addition, they are equally poised to provide through SARs, information that may benefit the mission of state regulatory agencies.

FinCEN analysts read and reviewed each of the 641 SARs filed by insurance companies between May 2, 2006 and May 1, 2007. The majority of SARs filed by unique corporate entities were produced in Massachusetts, New York, and Ohio. The residences of the majority of the individuals who were the subjects of these SARs were located in New York, California, Florida, and New Jersey.

Filers categorized over half of the subjects as policyholders of either the insured, the beneficiary, the payer, or the applicant. The next largest category of subjects was the applicant or owner of an annuity.

Consistent with data from all other financial services industries, insurance company filers most commonly cited "BSA/Money Laundering/Structuring" as the characterization of suspicious activity. Structuring, where larger transactions are broken into smaller exchanges, is consistent with an attempt to avoid currency reporting requirements.

The data revealed some potential trends in illicit activity. Some of the typologies evidenced in the narratives appeared very similar to classical examples of the money laundering stages of layering and integration.[1] For example, subjects sometimes used multiple cash equivalents (e.g., cashier's checks and money orders) from different banks and money services businesses to make policy or annuity payments, and then cashed out the insurance products to potentially disguise the original source of the funds. Also, some customers seemed unusually willing to incur significant penalties for surrendering their annuities before full term.

FinCEN agrees that both the insurance regulators and industry will benefit from a more industry-specific format for reporting suspicious activity. Currently, insurance industry SARs are being filed on the SAR-SF, which was designed for the Securities and Futures industry. The Suspicious Activity Report by Insurance Companies Notice and Request for Comment was published in the Federal Register on November 3, 2005.[2]

FinCEN has instructed insurance filers to add "SAR-IC" after the name of the institution (Part IV, Field 36) and begin the narrative with the term, "Insurance SAR" (Part VI).[3] This study found that some filers did not follow these instructions, thus hindering the identification of those filings as insurance SARs. Additionally, some filers include disclaimers in narratives. Disclaimers add no value to the SAR narrative and should be omitted.

---

1. Money laundering is a well-thought out process accomplished in three stages:
    Placement: Requires physically moving and placing the funds into financial institutions or the retail economy. Depositing structured amounts of cash into the banking sector, and smuggling currency across international borders for further deposit, are common methods for placement.
    Layering: Once the illicit funds have entered the financial system, multiple and sometimes complex financial transactions are conducted to further conceal their illegal nature, and to make it difficult to identify the source of the funds or eliminate an audit trail. Purchasing monetary instruments (traveler's checks, banks drafts, money orders, letters of credit, securities, bonds, etc.) with other monetary instruments, transferring funds between accounts, and using wire transfers facilitate layering.
    Integration: The illicit funds re-enter the economy disguised as legitimate business earnings (securities, businesses, real estate). Unnecessary loans may be obtained to disguise illicit funds as the proceeds of business loans

2. *See Notice and Request for Comments, Suspicious Activity Report by Insurance Companies*, 70 FR 66895 (November 3, 2005). See also *Release of Revised Suspicious Activity Reports*, 72 FR 23891 (May 1, 2007), indicating a delay to implement the effective date of the form due to the recently implemented data quality initiatives

3. See Frequently Asked Questions, Anti-Money Laundering Program and Suspicious Activity Reporting Requirements for Insurance Companies at
    http://www.fincen.gov/insurance_companies_faq.html.

Background

The USA PATRIOT Act, by expanding the definition of financial institutions, authorized FinCEN to promulgate regulations concerning anti-money laundering regulations and SAR filing requirements for certain segments of the insurance industry. The SAR regulation for insurance companies, which became effective on May 2, 2006, does not apply to all insurance companies.[4] The regulation established a SAR filing requirement only for those insurance companies that issue or underwrite specified "covered" products - a term defined to include: a permanent life insurance policy, other than a group life insurance policy; an annuity contract, other than a group annuity contract; and any other insurance product with cash value or investment features.[5]

This is the third FinCEN study of SARs filed on transactions involving insurance companies and insurance products. A report issued in May 2007 provided a summary of SARs filed in the 10-year period prior to May 2006 by all types of financial institutions regarding suspicious transactions involving insurance companies, insurance agents, and insurance brokers.[6] A report issued in February 2003 provided a summary of SARs filed between 1996 and 2002 by all types of financial institutions regarding transactions specifically involving life insurance products.[7] The current study highlights findings in an analysis of SARs filed within a timeframe that is shorter, relative to the previous studies. This study, however, considered a wider range of factors relevant to the reporting of suspicious activity involving insurance companies and insurance products. The findings and analyses in this report are intended to give insurance companies and other financial institutions broader insight into and different perspectives on the quality of insurance-related SARs, specifically, and on the effectiveness of SAR reporting programs, generally

---

4. 31 C.F.R. § 103.16.
5. 31 C.F.R. § 103.16(a)(4).
6. *The SAR Activity Review, Trends, Tips and Issues,* Issue # 11 (May 2007).
7. *The SAR Activity Review, Trends, Tips and Issues,* Issue #5 (May 2003).

Methodology

FinCEN used Bank Secrecy Act (BSA) database tools to retrieve all SARs filed by insurance companies and/or insurance carriers from May 2, 2006 to May 1, 2007, the first year after the mandatory suspicious activity reporting requirement for certain segments of the insurance industry. Since a dedicated SAR form for insurance companies has not yet been released for use, FinCEN instructed insurance companies to file on FinCEN Form 101: *Suspicious Activity Report by the Securities and Futures Industries*, adding "SAR-IC" in field 36, *Name of financial institution or sole proprietorship*,[8] and to begin the narrative field with the term, "Insurance SAR."[9]

During the period covered for this study, filers submitted 12,398 reports on Form 101. Of these, 322 notated insurance SARs.[10] However, a review of all 12,398 SAR-SFs, and the 864 distinct filer names, identified an additional 279 records filed by insurance companies. In order to provide complete feedback to the insurance industry, this study includes all 601 of these insurance company filings, with the result that some of the analysis includes uncovered products. Additionally, filers used Treasury Form TD F 90-22.47: *Suspicious Activity Report*, to file 40 SARs by or on behalf of insurance companies.[11] This study includes these reports, thus bringing the total number of SARs analyzed to 641. FinCEN analysts grouped the 641 SARs by filer, and then grouped the filers by their ultimate parent company. This study does not include joint SAR filings done by investment companies handling annuities or SARs filed by banks related to insurance products or agents.

---

8. Various BSA filing systems truncate Field 36 after the first 25, 30, or 35 characters. The long names of many insurance companies makes it impossible to see everything entered in Field 36. However, of the 50 SAR-SFs with some portion of "SAR-IC" visible in Field 36, all but one filer also identified the record as an insurance SAR in the narrative.

9. http://www.fincen.gov/insurance_companies_faq.html.

10. The analysis did not include three SAR-SFs filed by a non-insurance company, which both included "SAR-IC" in the name field and began the narrative with "Insurance SAR," but contained no descriptions of insurance-related activity.

11. SAR filings on TD F 90-22.47 by, or on behalf of, insurance companies were isolated by searching the database for key insurance-related terms, such as "insurance" or "annuity," and then seeing which of these were filed by insurance companies.

Research & Analysis

The filings retrieved for the time period covered by this study encompass 641 known records using FinCEN Form 101 (SAR-SF) and form TD F 90-22.47 (SAR-DI). Various tables representing data for each of the two record types combined follow.

Filings by Month[12]

GRAPH 1

Insurance Industry Suspicious Activity Reports
May 2, 2006 – May 1, 2007

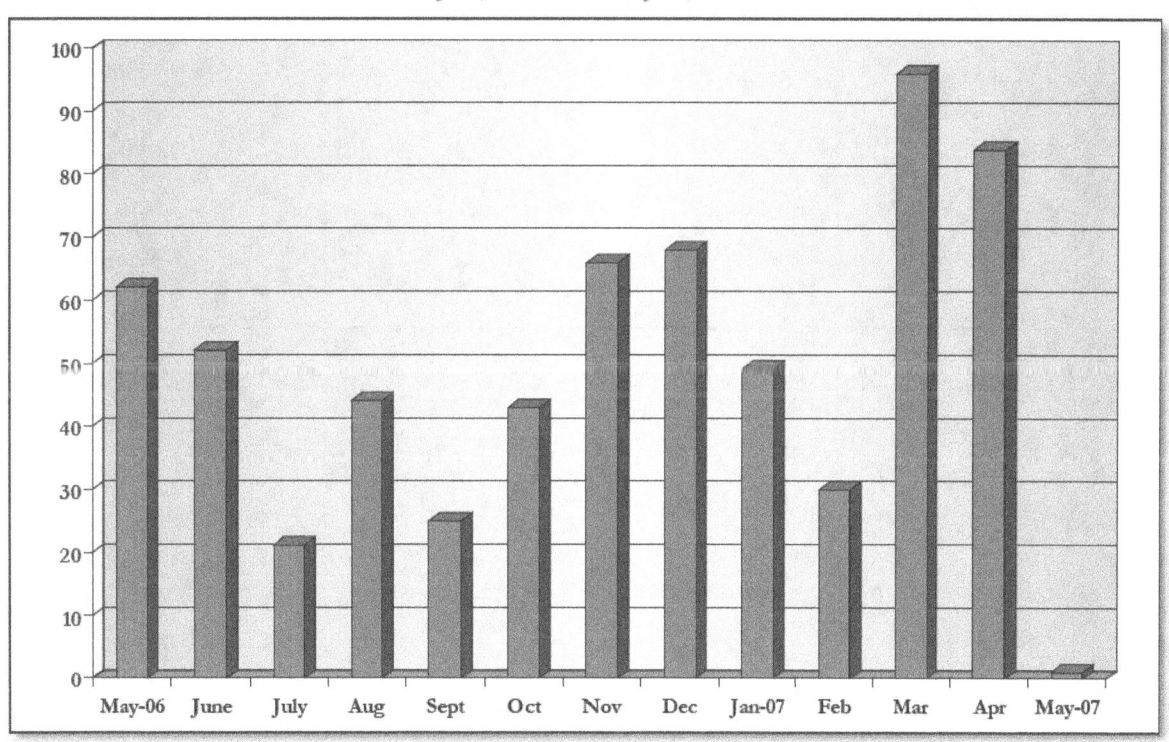

---

12. The single filing for the thirteenth month listed represents only the first day of May 2007 -- the date that completes the full one-year cycle.

Filings decreased in July and September 2006, and again in February 2007. This was followed by a sizeable increase in filings in March and April 2007. As this is only the first year of recorded mandatory filings, FinCEN will continue to study these and future filings to identify more specific filing trends. Preliminary analysis of filing rates for the six months after May 1, 2007 shows another decrease in filings for May and June 2007, and a significant spike in filings in October 2007. In general, the pattern reflects an overall steady increase in the number of SARs submitted by the insurance industry.

GRAPH 2

Insurance Industry Suspicious Activity Reports
May 2, 2007 – Oct 31, 2007

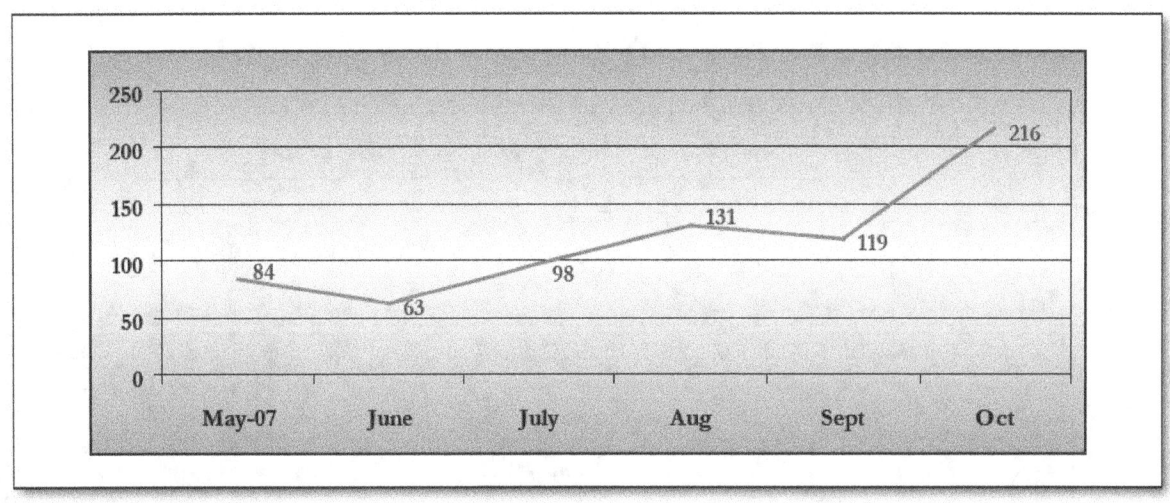

Filer Locations

Eighty-four unique entities from twenty-six states and Puerto Rico filed the SARs reviewed for this study. The following three locations, combined, accounted for more than 51 percent of the 641 SARs filed: Massachusetts (27.92 percent), New York (13.41 percent), and Ohio (10.45 percent).

GRAPH 3

Insurance Industry SAR Filers
by States & Territories

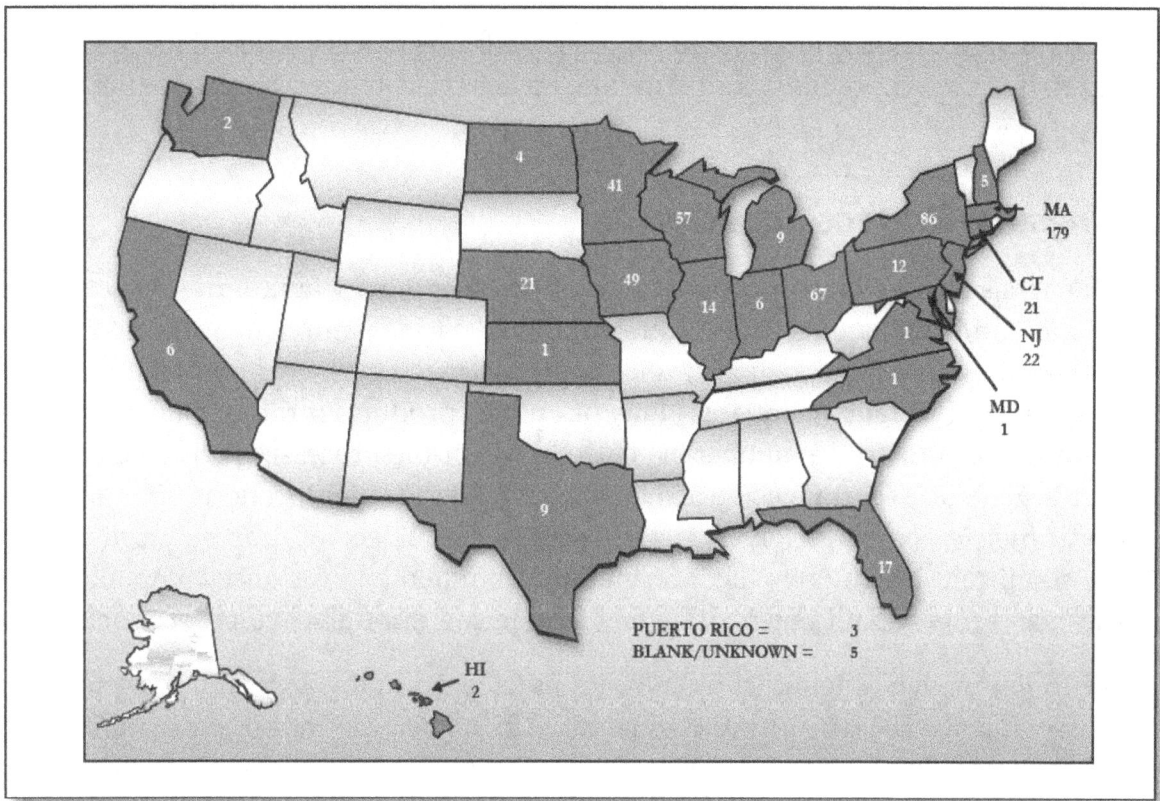

Massachusetts led as the state with the highest SAR volume as a result of the sizeable number of reports made by one firm, which, along with reports filed by companies owned by that firm's parent, made up slightly more than 22 percent of all records filed during the one-year period. Massachusetts insurance companies submitted 179 SARs through seven distinct entities.

Similarly, while companies in New York and Ohio filed SARs through multiple entities, a single firm in each state filed the majority of SARs. This was also the case for Wisconsin, ranked fourth among filing locations. For that state, five separate insurance carriers, through one entity, generated 88 percent of filings for the twelve-month period. Unlike in Massachusetts, the Wisconsin-based firm was not affiliated with other companies in and/or from the state during the same time frame.

The SAR filing volume for some institutions may be attributable to the diversified products and services they offer. Many companies have investment arms or broker-dealers with established AML programs. These programs already may cover a related aspect of their life insurance or annuity business (such as a broker-dealer) and could easily have been adapted for the covered products. An established AML program for their investment arm also may have been extended to include the covered products.

Filings by Subject Location

Past analysis has shown that certain types of fraud or money laundering may be recorded and/or initiated in one location, but take place in another. Suspected fraud or money laundering through insurance company products is primarily detected after the fact. Insurance companies may offer their products through a number of distribution channels in a number of states, however the processing unit and service center is generally centralized in one location. While the filer locations offer a valid analytic metric, comparatively or by themselves, the subject location may provide more significant insight(s) to the information submitted by insurance companies or insurance carriers about potential money laundering through covered products.

The following tables reflect subject locations as listed in the SARs retrieved for this assessment. The 641 insurance-related SARs named 773 individuals and/or businesses as subjects. The top five states for those 773 entities, based on addresses provided in the reports, include New York (173 or 22.38 percent), California (148 or 19.16 percent), Florida (45 or 6 percent), New Jersey (43 or 6 percent), and Texas (43 or 6 percent).

GRAPH 4

Insurance Industry SAR Subjects
by States & Territories

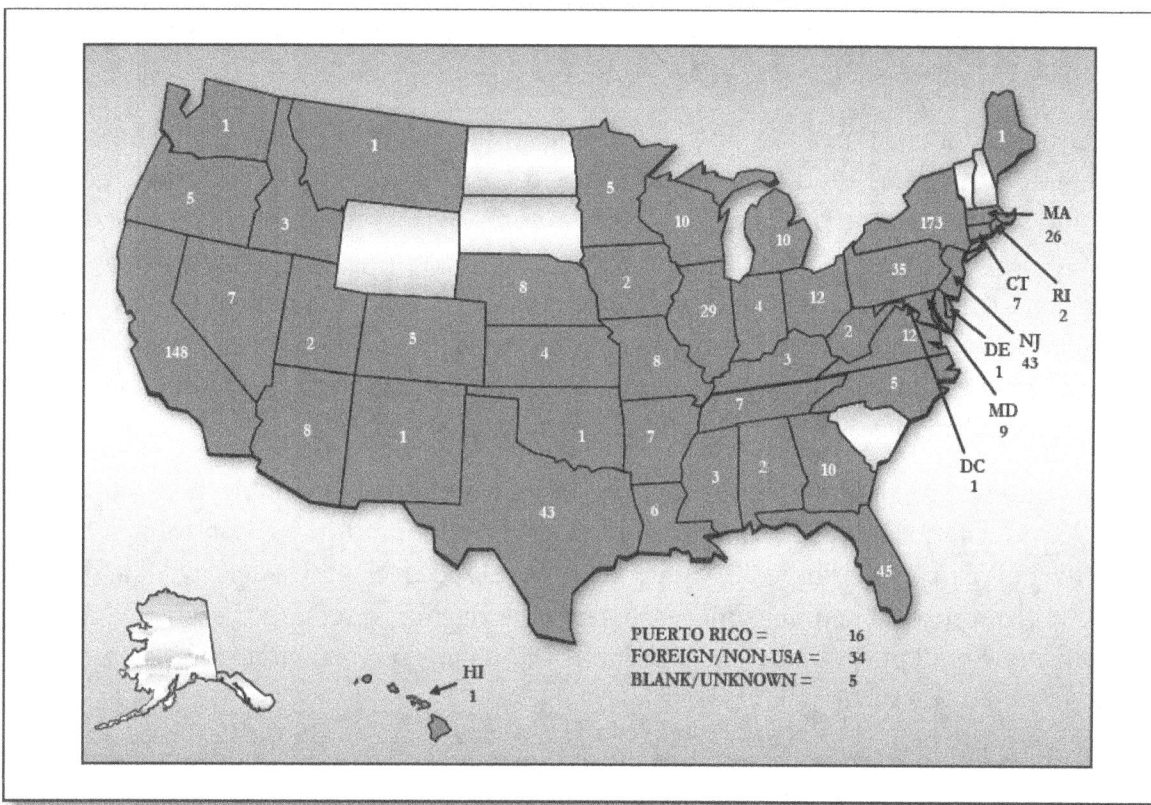

Insurance companies provided Massachusetts in the filing address in 103 of the 173 instances where the subject address was listed as New York. For these same 173 instances, 37 filers noted New York as their filing location. Filers located in California identified New York as the subjects' state in 53 of the 148 instances, followed by Iowa (25), and then Massachusetts (15). Only one California filer listed its own state as the filer and subject address location. This type of dissimilar relationship between filing state and subject address state is also reflected in the filings for Florida, New Jersey, Texas, Pennsylvania, and Illinois.

Filings by Subject Occupation, Type of Business or Relation to Insurance Company

Individuals accounted for the majority of listed subjects in the SARs; however, filers noted a few as business entities and, in some cases, identified a family's trust fund or retirement plan.

Approximately 65 percent of the subjects found in the 641 SARs were either: a) associated with some kind of business (named or un-named) or occupation[13]; b) identified by a job title, profession or other reference (Physician, Attorney, Restaurant Owner, Retired, etc.); or c) identified by a business name or the nature of the business if the subject was listed as a company. Thirty-five percent of the provided subject names contained no accompanying occupation[14] while others (included in those identified previously) were characterized in more general terms such as Owner Unknown Business, Partner, President, and others.

In an attempt to glean potential trends, this study divides the subjects of the 641 filings into categories based in part on their occupation and in part on their relationship to the insurance or investment product involved in the transaction. The data is derived from several sources on the SAR-SF: the narrative section (Part VI), Field 7 (*"Occupation or Type of Business"*), and Field 19 (*"Is this individual/business associated/ affiliated with the reporting financial institution?"*).

The study characterizes the subjects based on their relationship to the insurance products. These include different instances and combinations of the following roles: policyholder, beneficiary, insured, annuity owner, caregivers, and payers for other parties' annuities and policies.

The categories also include insurance insiders such as present or former employees of some insurance-related entity, including agents, brokers and sales representatives, and gatekeepers whose occupations give them direct responsibility to manage or guide money for others, such as accountants, lawyers and financial consultants.[15]

---

13. Percentage reflects entries in Field 7 (*Occupation or Type of Business*) only.

14. Percentage reflects non-entries in Field 7 (*Occupation or Type of Business*) only.

15. For the purposes of this study, a gatekeeper does not include: insurance insiders or CEOs, owners, and non-financial managers of non-finance-related firms. Based on the limited information available in SARs, analysis could not demonstrate that individuals in these positions actually managed or directed money.

Table 1 includes a summary of the numbers of SARs that contain subjects in the previously described roles.

TABLE 1

Categorization of Subjects Identified in SAR Narratives	
Role of Subject(s) Identified in Narratives	**SARs**
Life Policy Applicants, Beneficiaries, Insureds, Payers, and Caregivers	355
Annuity Owners or Applicants	197
Insurance Insiders	69
No Role of Subject Described or Identified	47
Gatekeepers	23

The following should be noted regarding this data:

First, this data does not compare directly with the occupational data derived solely from *Field 7* (*"Occupation or Type of Business"*) on the SAR form. Filers sometimes leave *Field 7* blank. Filers also sometimes provide information in narratives that is different from the information they provided in *Field 7*.

Second, the subject(s) for the purposes of these statistics are not necessarily the subject(s) whose information appears in *Part I* of either the SAR-DI or SAR-SF. The subjects for the purposes of these statistics are those whose activities were characterized in the narrative as being suspicious. For example, a filing may list one *subject* in *Part I*; however, its narrative may describe suspicious activities conducted by, or on behalf of, more individuals or entities.

Third, this data does not directly compare with other information collected on the SAR form with reference to the specific instruments involved in the reported transactions, as discussed *infra*. For example, analysis identified 225 filings that involved annuities, however, Table 1 shows 197 filings that named an annuity owner or applicant as a subject in the narrative, based on a relationship to an annuity. There are fewer annuity owners and applicants than annuity filings, because some narratives placed more emphasis on a gatekeeper or insurance insider as the one whose suspicious activities were being characterized. The roles of the subjects in these cases would be classified as insurance insiders or gatekeepers even though the SAR may have involved an annuity.

Tables 2 through 5 contain further breakdowns of the categories of roles played by subjects in Table 1. These subcategories are based on information contained in the narrative; however, several roles, like policy holder, are generic. A subject characterized or described in a manner consistent with the role of policy holder in a narrative does not mean that he/she was neither the insured nor beneficiary. In many instances, the narrative simply did not elaborate further on the subject's/subjects' role(s). As FinCEN enters into information-sharing arrangements with state insurance regulators, SAR information of the nature appearing in Table 4 (*Insurance Insiders*) can be anticipated to be of particular use in safety and soundness examinations.

TABLE 2

Policy Applicants, Beneficiaries, Holders, Insured, Payers, and Caregivers	
Role of Subject Identified by the Narrative	*SARs*
Policy Holder	195
Policy Holder/Insured	73
Policy Holder/Beneficiary	23
Policy Applicant	21
Beneficiary - Viatical Sale[16]	19[17]
Payer for the policy	15
Policy Holder/Non-Beneficiary	4
Policy Holder/Non-Insured	4
Caregiver for Accountholder	1
Total	**355**

16. A viatical is a contractual arrangement to purchase a life insurance policy from a terminally ill policy holder for a percentage of the face value. Viaticals are not covered products under the insurance rule. However, insurance companies may voluntarily file SARs and report suspicious activities that they wish to bring to law enforcement's attention whether or not they involve products specifically covered under the rule.

17. The actual number of SARs involving beneficiaries of viatical sales is better characterized as four rather than 19. One filer filed seventeen SARs on transactions from the same viatical settlement. Sixteen of these were filed on the beneficiaries of the settlement, and one was filed on the settlements company. These 16 filings would better be considered as one filing with 16 subjects.

TABLE 3

Annuity Owners and Applicants	
Role of Subject Identified by the Narrative	**SARs**
Annuity Owner	174
Annuity Applicant	23
Total	**197**

TABLE 4

Insurance Insiders	
Role of Subject Identified by the Narrative	**SARs**
Agent	48
Unspecified	5
Viatical Settlements Company	4[18]
Insurance Broker	8
Unlicensed Agent	4
District Sales Manager	1
CFO	1
Treasurer	1
Total	**72**

---

18. Three of the four filings mentioned the same viatical settlements company.

TABLE 5

Gatekeepers	
Role of Subject Identified by the Narrative	*SARs*
Attorney	10
Financial Advisor	3
Accountant	5
Policy Holder	2[19]
Total	**20**

___

19. In three filings, a gatekeeper was actually the policy holder.

Characterizations of Suspicious Activity[20]

GRAPH 5

Characterizations of Suspicious Activity Identified in SARs
Filed by Insurance Companies
May 2, 2006 – May 1, 2007

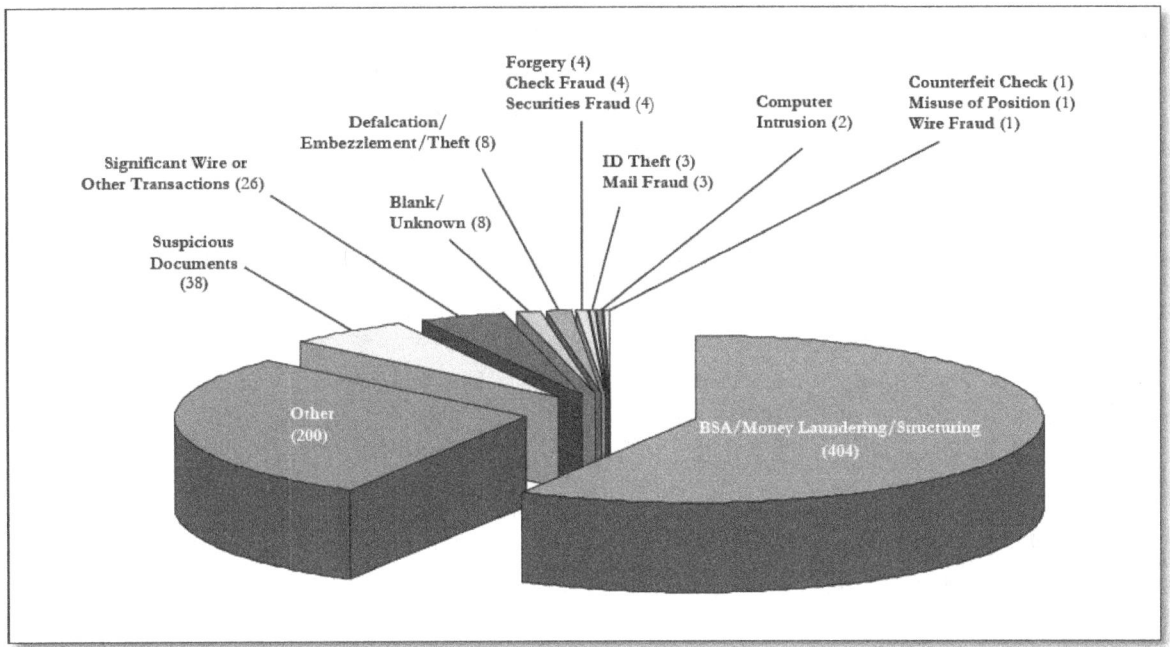

The most commonly listed Characterizations of Suspicious Activity (in whole or in part) were *BSA/Money Laundering/Structuring* and *Other* – the aggregated totals of which accounted for 85 percent of all reported suspected illicit activity.

Comparing the degree to which these suspected illicit activities were reported by the insurance industry during the filing period for this study, against the rates for the same suspected illicit activities as listed by SAR filers overall, cumulatively since the inception of each record type, the top two characterizations reflect those which also are reported on the Casino and Card Club SARs. In an analogous fashion, Securities and Futures Industries records list Other as first among reported violations

---

20. In some cases, due to their same or similar nature, summary characterizations were combined. For example: Bank Secrecy Act/Structuring/Money Laundering (TD F 90-47.22) and Money Laundering/Structuring (FinCEN Form 101) are presented as BSA/Money Laundering/Structuring. When the same box on both forms (Other) or uniquely represented (Securities Fraud), the characterization remains unchanged.

and *Money Laundering/Structuring* as second. While *BSA/Structuring* and *Other* are ranked one and two on the insurance industry SARs, these summary characterizations are ranked one and three on records as furnished by depository institutions.

Admittedly, these characterizations are currently being provided on a form (and in some cases, forms, considering those filings made on other existing record types) not tailored for this particular industry.[21] The future landscape of suspicious activity reporting might change when data is collected on a dedicated industry-specific SAR. Once this data collection process begins, FinCEN should have a more accurate depiction of suspicious financial activity in the insurance industry.

---

21. Currently, insurance companies may also use FinCEN Form 8300, Reports of Cash Payment Over $10,000 Received in a Trade or Business, as a means of reporting potential suspicious activity by checking Box 1b on the form and may use the Comments section on page 2 of the form to provide any additional information relevant to the transaction. On October 31, 2005, FinCEN published Frequently Asked Questions (www.fincen.gov/newsrelease10312005.html) on Anti-Money Laundering Program and Suspicious Activity Reporting Requirements for Insurance Companies which instructed filers to continue to use Form 8300 as appropriate (including potential suspicious activity involving the reported transaction) and to use the appropriate SAR form to report suspicious activity involving covered products (See Question 10).

Significant Findings

Analysis of Narratives

Product Types

Table 6 categorizes the products that were involved in the suspicious activities described in the 641 SAR narratives.

TABLE 6

Classification of Products Reported in Suspicious Activities	
Class of Product	SARs Identifying Use of Each Product
Life Insurance	265
Annuities	225
Unspecified and Other Insurance Products	73
No Insurance Product Identified	48
Life Insurance - Viatical Settlements	23
Liability Insurance	7
Property Insurance	3
Health Insurance	1
Worker's Compensation Insurance	1

Annuities

The nature of annuities and their potential to be considered both insurance and investment products complicated attempts during this study to differentiate annuities sold by insurance companies as insurance products from those annuities that qualify solely as investment products that happened to be sold by insurance companies.

The SAR narratives reference annuities in the manner portrayed in Table 7. Because many SAR narratives did not contain details about the features of the products described as annuity accounts or contracts, analysis could not determine whether the products were variable or fixed annuities. Analysis determined that 126 of the 251 SARs were intended to be Insurance SARs. In most of these cases, the insurance company provided the confirmation. Because the filers of the remaining 125 SARs did not follow both parts of the Insurance SAR filing instructions (indicating "SAR-IC" after the name of the institution and beginning the narrative with "Insurance SAR"), the filing status could not be further identified.

TABLE 7

SARs Filed By Insurance Companies Involving Annuities			
Instrument	SARs	Confirmed Insurance Filing	Unknown
Annuity Contract	98	46	52
Variable Annuity	78	36	42
Fixed Annuity	39	33	6
Annuity Account	36	11	25
Total	251	126	125

Life Insurance Policies

Insurance companies filed 265 SARs with narratives that characterized suspicious activity involving life insurance policies, of which 23 identified suspicious viatical settlements. Table 8 shows a breakdown of the types of life insurance policies that were part of the suspicious activity characterized in the 242 SAR filings.

TABLE 8

Suspicious Activity Reports Involving Life Insurance Policies	
Characterization of Life Insurance Policy	*SARs*
Life Insurance Policy	147
Universal Life Insurance Policy	39
Variable Life Insurance Policy	28
Whole Life Insurance Policy	28
Term Life Insurance Policy	27
Life Insurance Policy with a Paid-up Additional Rider	10
Variable Universal Life Insurance Policy	8
Variable Universal Life Policy – Group	4
Variable Life Insurance Policy – Corporate-Owned	3

Table 9 shows a breakdown of the types of policies that were tied to the viatical settlements described in the other 23 SAR filings.

TABLE 9

Suspicious Activity Reports Involving Viatical Settlements	
Policy Tied to Settlement	**SARs**
Term Life Insurance Policy	19
Life Insurance	2
Variable Life Insurance Policy	1
Whole Life Insurance Policy	1

The fact that one company filed seventeen SARs on a single viatical settlement of a term life policy distorts the total number of life insurance filings with narrative references to viatical settlements. One hundred forty-nine reports used generic terms, such as "life insurance" or "life policy," when naming the policy that was involved in the underlying suspicious activity. Another 46 identified term life policies, and 44 named different types of variable life policies.

Filings Involving Non-covered Products

Nine insurance companies filed a total of fourteen SARs solely involving non-covered products. FinCEN's analysis identified two additional SARs of this type, which were filed on behalf of two other insurance companies. Twelve of the sixteen filings related to term life policies. Of the remaining four, one involved a health insurance policy; a second involved a group variable universal life plan; a third involved a mobile home policy; and a forth involved a surety bond, a notary public bond, a power of attorney bond, a liability policy, a professional liability policy, and a worker's compensation policy. Table 10 indicates the reasons cited in the narratives for the filings.

TABLE 10

Categorization of SARs Involving Non-covered Products	
Reasons for The Filing	**SARs**
Insurance Fraud	5
OFAC Blocking Report	3
Multiple Money Orders or Checks Used for Payment or Initial Purchase	2
Significant Transactions (Wire or Other) Without Economic Purpose	2
Media Reports of Illegal Activity	1
Money Laundering	1
Potential Terrorist Financing	1

The five instances of insurance fraud reflected in Table 10 resulted from individuals who supplied fraudulent information on applications for term life policies. As set forth in FinCEN regulations,[22] an insurance company is not required to report instances of suspected insurance fraud unless the company has reason to believe that the false or fraudulent submission of information relates to money laundering or terrorist financing. One narrative characterized potential terrorist financing when a subject questioned if his term life and accidental death and dismemberment policies would pay if he were killed in a suicide bombing. This was one of three filings that involved this scenario and potential terrorist financing.[23] The presence of a small number of filing(s) potentially related to the financing of terrorism should not be construed to mean that term life policies constitute a significant money-laundering or terrorist-financing threat.

---

22. 31 C.F.R. § 103.16(d).

23. The other two filings are not included in the counts in Table 10 because they involved other covered products.

What generated the filings?

Because the SAR-SF form is not tailored to the insurance industry, analysts for this study used the narratives to attempt to identify the exact reason for each filing. Using the list of characterizations of suspicious activities in the proposed dedicated SAR form for insurance companies as a reference, analysts divided the filings into categories for statistical purposes. Table 11 includes a breakdown of the reasons derived from information in the narratives for the 641 filings. Insurance companies filed 636 of the 641 reports, and FinCEN systems generated the remaining five reports, on behalf of insurance companies, as a result of OFAC blocking reports.

TABLE 11

Narrative-Derived Reasons For Filings	
Reasons For Filing	**SARs**
Multiple Money Orders or Checks Used for Payment or Loan Repayment	274
Early/Excessive Borrowing	94
BSA/Structuring/Money Laundering	84
Early Policy Termination/Annuity Redemption	73
Significant Transactions (Wire Or Other) Without Economic Purpose	67
Commercial Watch List	27
Insurance Fraud	27
Subject of Law Enforcement Investigation	26
Unusual Payment Method	26
Government Watch List[24]	20
Identity Theft	20
Unusual Viatical Sales	20
Suspicious Documents or ID Presented	18

---

24. This characterization appearing in SAR narratives and commonly used by industry filers may refer to names found in various lists issued by government agencies.

Media Reports of Illegal Activity	17
Little or No Product Performance Concern	14
Suspicious Transfer, or Loan to, or Payments by Unrelated Third Party	11
Unusual Use of Free-Look Provision	10
Tax Evasion	9
Mail or Email Fraud	8
Self Dealing/Embezzlement	7
Potential Terrorist Financing	6
Unusual Surrender Payment Request	6
Early Request For Refund of Premiums Paid in Advance	5
Check Fraud	4
Fraudulent Documents Presented by Agent	4
Counterfeit Instruments	3
False Statements	3
Financial Advisor or Parent Company Referral	3
Forgery	2
Alleged Prime-Bank Scheme	1
Attempt to Avoid Filing IRS Form W-9	1
Compliance Review	1
Computer Intrusion	1
Internal Audit of an Agent	1
IRS Audit of Subject	1
Refusal to Provide Verifying Information	1
Suspicious Questions About BSA Reporting Requirements	1
Wire Fraud	1

The first four entries in the table relate to several potential trends identified in the narrative analysis.

Potential Trends:

Use of cash equivalents from multiple sources

Owners of high cash businesses used multiple cash equivalents from different banks and money services businesses to pay into policies and annuities.

In one case, an insurer reported the owner of a landscaping business who paid the premiums on a universal life insurance policy with multiple money orders of no more than $1,000 each, some purchased on the same day at different post offices, or on separate visits to the same post office, creating the appearance of structuring.

Another company filed a report on a woman who made multiple structured premium payments totaling $100,000, with cashier's checks and money orders with values from $200 to $9,000, "for the purchase of what are, essentially, lump sum premium annuity products."

A significant number of filings involved individuals paying into policies or annuities, some with cash equivalents from multiple sources. Repeated loans were taken against the policies or annuities or the policies and annuities were surrendered to the economic detriment of the annuity owner.

Large dollar withdrawals made shortly after the policy/contract was issued

One such SAR described a man who purchased a $2.5 million annuity with a check from a corporation unknown to the filer, claiming the funds were lottery winnings. He then withdrew more than $2.1 million within nine months, despite a ten percent penalty, claiming he wanted the money to fund a business acquisition.

Another filing described a business owner who opened a pair of variable annuities totaling over $550,000 in February 2006, and added over $720,000 to the annuities before the end of June 2006. From February to July 2006, the annuity owner made almost $550,000 in surrenders, incurring more than $39,000 in penalties.

Surrenders that only incurred tax-related penalties

Insurance companies filed several SARs related to the surrenders of annuities, which had return-of-premium guarantees. The only penalties were tax related. In many of these instances, the annuity owner surrendered the annuity more than one year after purchasing it.

In one example, a customer purchased a variable annuity in 2000, depositing $195,000 for tax-deferred retirement savings. From 2001 to 2007, she made 63 withdrawals totaling $99,000, with no surrender charges, but incurring tax liability for early withdrawal.

Potential Monitoring Practices:

The "Narrative-Derived Reasons For Filings" listed in Table 11 indicate that some insurance companies are monitoring for potential money laundering "red flags" involving their products. While it is not illegal to use multiple money orders or checks (the primary means described in the narratives) to pay premiums or repay loans, the use of several from multiple sources or multiple locations could indicate the layering stage of money laundering. Early or excessive borrowing against a policy or contract could be an attempt to get illicit funds back into circulation (the integration stage) after the funds were placed into the financial system through the insurance product.

Terminating a policy or annuity shortly after issuance also may indicate possible money laundering, especially if the policy holder or contract holder is willing to incur potential tax consequences or high surrender charges. The ten day free look provision in some insurance products may be particularly susceptible to money laundering since it provides an easy means for the money launderer to place the illicit proceeds into the financial system, and then cancel the contract and integrate the funds back into the mainstream through a newly issued check from the insurance company.

It should be noted that simply exercising a provision of the contract, such as the ten day free look or a loan option, is not necessarily suspicious activity. Rather, these transactions should be reviewed for anything that appears suspicious about the actual transaction. For example, a policy holder opens an annuity with a high premium amount and then immediately takes a loan for nearly the entire premium amount and asks that the proceeds be sent to a third party. Or, an annuity is opened with a series of money orders totaling a significant amount and then the ten day free look option is exercised with instructions to send a check to an unrelated third party.

Given the most commonly described reasons for filing as provided in the narratives (Table 11), discovery of the suspicious activity is more likely to occur once the policy or annuity has been issued by the insurance company and not necessarily at the agent or broker level. It should be noted, however, that attempts to launder money through insurance products can occur at the point the customer is in direct contact with the agent or broker, such as when payments are made through cash equivalents or multiple money orders. Consequently, an insurance company's ability to detect suspicious activity will be aided by agents and brokers that remain alert to suspicious activity involving the products they sell.

Other Filings of Note:

The most prolific filer of the insurance companies submitted 143 reports, 138 from its main subsidiary. Although the names of two of the subsidiaries (accounting for 141 SAR-SFs) were truncated, 108 of the company's filings began the narrative with "Insurance SAR." Of the 143 SAR-SFs filed, 108 dealt with life insurance, 19 with annuities, and 10 reported matches to confidential government lists. One hundred twenty-nine of the reports involved the use of money orders to pay premiums or pay back loans.

Another company filed 17 of its 41 SARs on employees of a landscaping company, who tried to open variable annuity contracts with their employer-sponsored individual retirement accounts. All of the employees reported in these SARs had fraudulent Social Security numbers.

Quality of SAR Filings

One of the main purposes of this study is to evaluate the overall quality of filings by insurance companies, due to their new role as SAR filers, and identify areas for reporting improvements. FinCEN uses such analysis in part to identify areas on which to focus industry outreach and education efforts, and provide feedback such as the following.

Compliance with Instructions

Page three of the SAR-SF states that preparers should "provide a clear, complete and chronological narrative description" of the activity that resulted in the filing. The instructions provide guidance lettered a.-v. to help the preparer accomplish this. Items a.-v. of the narrative instructions are meant to serve as a checklist and not as individual questions for filers to answer. Six different insurance companies filed a total of forty-eight SARs with narratives that contained the individual letters found in the instructions followed by answers to them. Preparing a narrative in this manner makes it less clear and comprehensible. Law enforcement officials who read these narratives must often refer back to the individual items. Filers should avoid responding to items a.-v as if they were individual questions.

Several insurance companies filed multiple SARs with single subjects on the same suspicious activity. Six insurance companies filed multiple SARs with a single subject on the same instance of a suspicious activity. One insurance company filed 17 SAR-SFs on a single claim from a viatical settlement. All 17 filings had the same narrative that described the same transaction. Another insurance company filed five single-subject SARs on the same transaction. In these instances, the filers should have filed single SARs listing the multiple subjects.

Filing Errors

Nine different insurance companies filed a total of thirty-five SARs using the SAR-DI, contrary to FinCEN's instructions. The regulations that went into effect on May 2, 2006 require insurance companies to file SAR-SFs on covered insurance activities. Of these nine filers, four also filed SAR-SFs on insurance-related transactions.

FinCEN identified at least 21 SARs with additional errors not previously discussed in this section. In 17 of these filings, the dollar amount listed in Field 21(*"Total amount involved in suspicious activity"*) of the SAR-SF did not match the amount related to suspicious transactions characterized in the narrative. In many cases, the filer simply placed zero in the field, or left it blank. In other instances, the filer questioned money entering a policy or annuity but only identified the dollar amount that left the policy or annuity in the form of redemptions or loans. The narrative of one filing had several conflicting dates, including closing a policy before it was opened. At least one filing had an incorrect value for Field 20 (*"Date or date range of suspicious activity"*) that occurred after the date the report was filed. At least one preparer misspelled the filer's name and one SAR was filed without a narrative. It is critical that the information in a SAR filing be as accurate and complete as possible. FinCEN believes that a simple review of the prepared SAR would likely have allowed for correction by the filer; such effort would be much less than presumably already expended in the determination to file these particular SARS. FinCEN has previously provided suggestions for addressing common errors noted in suspicious activity reporting[25] as well as guidance on preparing a complete and sufficient SAR narrative.[26]

---

25. http://www.fincen.gov/SAR_Common_Errors_Web_Posting.html.

26. http://www.fincen.gov/sarnarrcompletguidfinal_112003.pdf.

Analysis identified other instances where data supplied by insurance companies appeared to be erroneous; this section only describes those errors that were both identified and could be corroborated.

Disclaimers about sources of funds when law enforcement investigations, media reports, or watch lists caused investigations that led to the filings

Insurance companies filed 52 reports that resulted from negative media reports, law enforcement investigations, and commercial or government watch lists. Nineteen of these 52 reports and four additional filings that did not result from negative media reports, contained disclaimers stating that the sources of funds used to make payments on insurance or annuity products may have come from illegal activities. Such disclaimers neither absolve insurance companies of monitoring and due diligence requirements nor provide them any protection. Disclaimers add no value to the SAR narrative and should be omitted.

Compliance with "SAR-IC" Guidelines

In guidance issued on May 31, 2006 (FIN-2006-G010),[27] FinCEN instructed insurance companies to file reports of suspicious activity using FinCEN Form 101, SAR-SF. The guidance also included instructions for identifying the filing as an insurance company SAR.

Precisely how these criteria were met, in whole or in part, based on those SARs reviewed for this study, are explained accordingly:

Filers correctly used the SAR-SF in approximately 94 percent of the reports submitted to FinCEN. The remainder utilized FinCEN Form TD F 90-22.47.

From May 2, 2006 to May 1, 2007, institutions filed 12,398 SAR-SF forms. Of these, insurance companies filed 601. Fifty of the 601 (8.3 percent) included "SAR-IC" in field 36. (Field 36 was truncated in 33 of these 50, from 14 distinct filers, but a truncated form of "SAR-IC" was still visible.) Field 36 was truncated[28] at or before the end of the company name in another 425 SAR-SFs (70.7 percent of all industry reports) filed by 48 insurance companies, so it is unknown how many of these reports included "SAR-IC." Of the 601 SAR-SFs filed by insurance companies, at least 148 reports (24.6 percent) from 29 distinct companies did not include "SAR-IC" in field 36.

---

27. www.fincen.gov/insurance_companies_faq.html.

28. The long-form names of many insurance companies made it impossible to see everything entered in to Field 36 – the last item of which may have, most likely, included "SAR-IC."

Of the 601 insurance company filings using the SAR-SF form, the narratives of 321 (53.4 percent) indicated that they were insurance SARs. Of those, 252 (41.9 percent) began the narrative field with the term "Insurance SAR." Another 69 (11.5 percent of the 601) of the insurance company filings started the narrative with some other indication that it was an insurance SAR, such as "SAR-IC," "This is an insurance SAR," or "This is an insurance company SAR."

Forty-nine insurance company SAR-SFs filed (8.15 percent) included "SAR-IC" with the financial institution name in Part IV of the form (line 36) and "Insurance SAR" in the first line of the narrative. Only one SAR-SF had "SAR-IC" in the name field, but no indicators in the narrative. Another 231 industry SAR-SFs (38.4 percent) met the narrative criteria and had Field 36 truncated at or before the end of the company name, and so may have met both criteria. Forty-one insurance company SAR-SFs met the narrative criteria, but did not have "SAR-IC" in Field 36, nor was it truncated at or before the end of the company name. Only one SAR-SF by an insurance company met the name criteria but did not include a statement at the beginning of the narrative. Eighty-five of the SAR-SFs (14.14 percent) in the study had no indication in the narrative that they were insurance SARs, failed to meet the name field criteria, and their name fields were not truncated.

The following tables provide additional detailed breakdowns of how institutions met filing criteria.

Total SAR-SFs (FinCEN Form 101) filed from May 2, 2006 to May 1, 2007	12,398
SAR-SFs filed by insurance companies (same period)	601
Depository Institution SARs (TD F 90-22.47) filed by insurance companies (during the same period)	40
Total SARs filed by insurance companies from May 2, 2006 to May 1, 2007	641

SAR-SFs that included "SAR-IC" or "SARIC" in Field 36	50*
Complete	17*
Truncated	33

* Does not include three non-insurance related SAR-SFs filed by a securities company that erroneously included the SAR-IC markings.

SAR-SFs with Field 36 truncated at or before end of name	425

SAR-SFs whose narratives indicate they are insurance SARs	321*
SAR-SFs that began narrative with "Insurance SAR"	252*
SAR-SFs that began narrative with some other indication they are insurance SARs	69

* Does not include three non-insurance related SAR-SFs filed by a securities company that erroneously included the SAR-IC markings.

SAR-SFs that included "SAR-IC" in Field 36, and began the narrative with "Insurance SAR," or some other indication it is an insurance SAR	49*

* Does not include three non-insurance related SAR-SFs filed by a securities company that erroneously included the SAR-IC markings.

SAR-SFs that:	
Met Both Criteria Exactly	45*
Did Not Meet Name-Field Criterion; Did Not Meet Narrative Criterion	85

* Does not include three non-insurance related SAR-SFs filed by a securities company that erroneously included the SAR-IC markings.

Overall, the quality of narratives furnished on the SARs retrieved for this assessment was good – especially considering the often complex nature of the transactions involved. Only one of the records retrieved for this study lacked a narrative.

Conclusions & Recommendations

The SARs reviewed for this study indicated that while there were fluctuations from month to month in the number filed by insurance companies, overall the volume has been increasing since the Insurance mandated suspicious activity reporting rule became effective on May 2, 2006. The analysis indicated that there were certain States and filers with the most filings during this period, although this is likely to change as the number of filings increase. Many of these filings could be attributed to the reporting patterns of particular entities and do not necessarily indicate money laundering vulnerabilities with the filing entity or the location of the filer or the subject.

Analysis of SAR narratives revealed that the most frequently identified subject of the suspicious activity, when such a designation was made, had a direct relationship to the policy or account (the applicant, insured party, beneficiary, etc.); less commonly reported were insurance insiders, such as an agent or broker, or someone serving in a gatekeeper role, such as an accountant or lawyer.

While the most common characterization of suspicious activity reported was BSA/Money Laundering/Structuring, a review of SAR narratives determined that the most commonly described suspicious activity involved the use of multiple money orders or checks for premium and loan payments, followed by early or excessive borrowing, structuring/money laundering, early termination of a policy or annuity and significant transaction with no apparent economic purpose. These patterns in part were detected due to the fact that FinCEN instructed insurance companies to file on a form, FinCEN Form 101, which was designed for the Securities and Futures Industry. Therefore, insurance companies use the narrative section to more accurately describe the actual suspicious activity being reported. As a result, with few exceptions, the quality of SAR narratives provided by insurance companies has been good.

Another notable finding in the study was the inclusion of filings involving viaticals, a non-covered product. The existence of such filings may indicate a concern among certain insurance companies about the mere practice of viatical sales and settlements and the potential for fraud rather than their use as a vehicle for money laundering. FinCEN will continue to analyze this reporting to see if it increases in significance.

Although insurance companies submitted 641 SARs in the one-year period following the effective date for mandated suspicious activity reporting, FinCEN expects the level and quality of filings to increase in the future as more institutions become familiar with the reporting obligations and understand the importance of the information to law enforcement.

Finally, when an industry is asked to meet a reporting requirement using reports not tailored to its industry, inconsistencies may exist in the way that reporting requirement is met. Such is the case with the use of the SAR-SF and other forms for reporting suspicious activity in the insurance industry. While most insurers did correctly file on the SAR-SF, some did not. Even when the correct form was used, some filers did not follow FinCEN guidance for identifying the report as an insurance SAR. FinCEN acknowledges the need to implement changes currently demonstrated by the proposed SAR-IC form to tailor the filing process to insurance companies, but in the interim it is important that filers continue to follow guidance previously published by FinCEN describing the proper method for correctly identifying the filing as an insurance SAR.

Appendix A

APPENDIX A – *Guidance, Rules and News Releases Regarding the Insurance Industry*

Following are links to previously released information, regarding the insurance industry and its responsibilities under the Bank Secrecy Act. All of the information listed below currently appears on FinCEN's website – http://www.fincen.gov.

Anti-Money Laundering Program and Suspicious Activity Reporting Requirements for Insurance Companies (Guidance) – March 20, 2008 (http://www.fincen.gov/fin-2008-g004.pdf)

Financial Crimes Enforcement Network: Amendment Regarding Financial Institutions Exempt from Establishing Anti-Money Laundering Programs (Final Rule) – January 11, 2008 (http://www.fincen.gov/FedReg-1-11-08.pdf)

Anti-Money Laundering Program and Suspicious Activity Reporting Requirements for Insurance Companies (Guidance) – May 31, 2006 (http://www.fincen.gov/insurance_companies_faq.pdf)

Requirement that Insurance Companies Report Suspicious Transactions (Final Rule) – November 3, 2005 (http://www.fincen.gov/sarforinsurancecompany.pdf)

Anti-Money Laundering Programs for Insurance Companies (Final Rule) – November 3, 2005 (http://www.fincen.gov/amlforinsurancecompany.pdf)

Suspicious Activity Report by Insurance Companies (Notice and Request for Comments) – November 3, 2005 (http://www.fincen.gov/sarcomments10312005.pdf)

Insurance Companies Required to Establish Anti-Money Laundering Programs and File Suspicious Activity Reports (News Release) – October 31, 2005 (http://www.fincen.gov/newsrelease10312005.pdf)

Anti-Money Laundering Programs for Insurance Companies (Correction to Notice of Proposed Rule) – November 12, 2002 (http://www.fincen.gov/fedreginsurance111202.pdf)

Requirement that Insurance Companies Report Suspicious Transactions (Notice of Proposed Rulemaking) – October 17, 2002 (http://www.fincen.gov/insurance_sar.pdf)

Anti-Money Laundering Programs for Insurance Companies (Notice of Proposed Rulemaking) – September 26, 2002 (http://www.fincen.gov/352insurance.pdf)

Appendix B

APPENDIX B - Law Enforcement Cases Relating to the Insurance Industry

Insurance Executive Sentenced In Embezzlement Scheme[29]

In a case initiated based on the filing of a SAR, a former high-ranking officer of an insurance firm, who was charged in a multiple-count federal indictment including counts of embezzling insurance premiums, falsifying records and filing false tax returns, has been sentenced to almost two years in prison for embezzling over $100,000 and filing a false tax return. The defendant pled guilty to one count of embezzlement and one count of filing a false federal tax return. The defendant also admitted to issuing company checks to himself and concealing the embezzlements. He said he used the money to pay gambling debts. The defendant has paid back all of the embezzled funds.

(Investigating Agencies: Federal Bureau of Investigation and Internal Revenue Service -- Criminal Investigation Division.)

Bank Secrecy Act Records Lead to Funds for Restitution in Insurance Fraud[30]

A series of CTRs proved crucial in identifying bank accounts used to hide proceeds obtained through insurance fraud. The fraud involved a contractor who misrepresented the number of workers in his temporary employment service. Authorities used BSA data to identify assets belonging to perpetrators.

---

29. The SAR Activity Review, Trends, Tips and Issues, Issue #11 (May 2007), page 32; http://www.fincen.gov/sarreviewissue11.pdf

30. The SAR Activity Review, Trends, Tips and Issues, Issue #10 (May 2006), page 23; http://www.fincen.gov/sarreviewissue10.pdf

The defendant owned and operated a company that provided temporary employees to businesses in a neighboring state. The company, which changed names a number of times in a span of five years, generally employed over 100 laborers, but only paid insurance premiums based on declarations to insurance companies that the company employed only a little more than 10 laborers.

The scheme primarily involved creating two separate companies on paper. One company would employ approximately 10 percent of the employees and the other the remaining 90 percent. An insurance policy would be purchased only for the small company. The companies had very similar names so that they were able to mislead businesses in the neighboring state into believing the policy covered all employees of both companies. Whenever an employee was injured, the company would either arrange to pay the injured worker to avoid filing a claim, or it would file a claim in the name of the covered company. Over the course of five years, the companies were able to defraud two insurance companies of millions of dollars in premiums.

In late 2005, the defendant was sentenced in U.S. District Court for his part in the scheme to defraud insurance companies of millions of dollars. His sentence included 108 months in prison, and he was ordered to pay in excess of $5 million in restitution to the two insurance companies.

Moreover, evidence at the defendant's trial showed that he was also engaged in an elaborate scheme to avoid paying taxes on profits from his employment service. BSA data also helped unravel this second scheme.

This scheme was accomplished by creating false business expenses and invoices from fictitious trucking companies. Money was moved from one company account to another, before converting it to currency by cashing checks at a grocery store. The defendant's company also used fictitious gasoline purchase invoices in its scheme.

The matter was turned over to the investigating arm of the state's Department of Insurance and ultimately to the U.S. Postal Inspection Service. Federal officers seized or placed under court ordered restraint numerous assets belonging to the defendant including cash, certificates of deposit, vehicles, airplanes, homes and personal assets. The total value of the assets seized approached the amount by which the insurance companies had been defrauded.

A Postal investigator said that by searching BSA information the Postal Service was able to identify two large bank accounts with a total balance of over half a million dollars. He also stated that these two accounts were the largest found belonging to the defendant. Authorities seized the funds in the accounts and designated it for restitution to the insurance companies.

(Investigating Agency: U.S. Postal Inspection Service)

www.FinCEN.gov